Original title:
The Jungle Upstairs

Copyright © 2025 Creative Arts Management OÜ
All rights reserved.

Author: Harrison Blake
ISBN HARDBACK: 978-1-80581-908-0
ISBN PAPERBACK: 978-1-80581-435-1
ISBN EBOOK: 978-1-80581-908-0

Nature's Heartbeat in the Eaves

In the rafters, critters play,
Squirrels dance and chirp away.
Their acrobatics, quite a sight,
A furry circus day and night.

A spider weaves a gleeful trap,
While mice give the cat a cheeky clap.
A thumping beat from the drywall,
Is it a jungle? Not at all!

Skylight Serenades

Sunbeams burst like popcorn drops,
As birds gather in rooftop hops.
They sing a tune of pure delight,
Creating chaos in the light.

A pigeon struts with clumsy flair,
While butterflies play tag in air.
With giggles shared by breeze and flower,
Nature's laugh, an hour after hour.

Where Dreams Meet the Vines

Lurking vines with sneaky grins,
Stretch to grab the passing winds.
Bouncing beetles, oh so spry,
Laugh at clouds that drift on by.

A lizard lounges, pillow-molded,
In a hammock, sunlight-gilded.
He snickers at the jumping bugs,
Sips nectar, gives the air a shrug.

Woven Whispers of the Loft

In the quiet, whispers twirl,
As the bats perform a swirl.
They're tiny pirates, soaring high,
With little eyepatches in the sky.

A cozy nook for goblins to nap,
With gossamer tents made from a scrap.
Their funny pranks make shadows dance,
In dreams, they swirl and prance.

Breaths of the Unseen Green

In shadows where the spiders twirl,
The dust bunnies perform a swirl.
A leaf slips down with a tiny squeak,
Where all the critters play hide and seek.

The curtains sway with a gentle gust,
While mice hold court, in them we trust.
A squirrel peeks from a corner bright,
Chasing dreams in the cheerful light.

The Ceiling Becomes a Canopy

With light bulbs glowing like fireflies,
Chasing shadows that dance and rise.
A wooden beam bears the weight of cheer,
Where whispered giggles from friends appear.

A paper crane flaps on a breeze,
While cats plot mischief among the leaves.
In sudden leaps and bounding grace,
They land on ledges, oh such a race!

Twilight in the Upper Thicket

At dusk, the shadows twist and bend,
As pillows join the fun to blend.
A blanket fort, a kingdom grand,
Where monsters are merely just fluff in hand.

With twinkling stars made of stickers bright,
Laughter echoes into the night.
Pirate ships sail in dainty dreams,
All while giggles float in streams.

Secrets Among the Beams

Whispers linger in dusty light,
A hidden world takes joyful flight.
The mice have maps to adventure's stash,
While secret notes cause giggles to clash.

Old toys gather in loopy trance,
In forgotten corners, they all prance.
A teddy bear conducts a show,
In this high-up land where silliness flows.

Whispers from the Canopy

In the trees above, a monkey grins,
Wearing a crown made of salad spins.
Squirrels debate the best nut to share,
Only to find that the cat's watching there.

Frogs on bandstands sing their tunes,
While snails hold races under the moons.
The laughter of leaves joins the fun,
Nature's party has only just begun.

Secrets Among Shadows

A raccoon whispers, 'Shh, don't you peek!'
He's hiding a treasure, a shiny old cheek.
While bats get tangled in their midnight games,
Hilarious antics, yet no one claims.

The grasshoppers hop like they own the place,
In a dance-off with ants, it's a wild space.
Each corner hides giggles, a secret throng,
Under the blanket of night, they belong.

Echoes of the Wild

Parrots squawk tales of bravado and cheese,
While turtles pretend they're racing the breeze.
The laughter of crickets fills all the nooks,
With frogs as the critics of nature's new books.

In the underbrush, a rooster's on break,
With dreams of grandeur and a big chocolate cake.
Echoes bounce back, teasing whispers play,
With every creature having their say.

Vines of Imagination

Vines twist and twirl, creating a stage,
Where chameleons act out their silliest rage.
With capes made of leaves, they take to the air,
While insects applaud, 'What a daring affair!'

A sloth provides timing, moving so slow,
Adding suspense to the wariest show.
In this green realm, laughter ignites,
Where fantasy blooms in whimsical sights.

Vines of the Forgotten Room

In corners dense, where dust balls rest,
    A lizard dressed in a tiny vest.
He juggles socks from laundry's foe,
While vines debate the way to grow.

The spider spins a web of cheer,
While mice throw parties with soda, oh dear!
A clock ticks backward, how absurd,
    It whispers secrets without a word.

Mysteries Above the Ceiling

A raccoon chef is stirring stew,
With acorns and a touch of dew.
Squirrels gossip, tails in a twist,
They plan a trip we can't resist.

An owl recites a bedtime tale,
As shadows dance in the moonlit veil.
Balloons float high, then pop with glee,
Who knew up here could be so free?

Echoes from the High Branches

The ceiling creaks, what could it be?
A cat in a top hat, fancy and free!
He taps his paw in rhythm divine,
And croons along with a beat-up line.

A parade of ants on a tightrope strung,
Their tiny feet beat like a drum that's rung.
With streamers made of shiny thread,
They march and giggle, then flee in dread.

Secrets in the Attic Air

Old trunks hold dreams with velvet hides,
While shadows cruise on mischievous rides.
A ghost with a wig tries to dance so bold,
While laughter echoes like stories retold.

Dust bunnies plot in a fluffy crew,
Wielding their spoons to stir up the brew.
With each thump and bump, the chaos grows,
In this attic, anything goes!

Songs of the Rafter Birds

High above in the beams,
Rafter birds plot their schemes.
With a chirp and a tweet,
They're tapping their feet.

They swoop in for a snack,
A cookie that's turned black.
They laugh as we frown,
In feathery gowns.

A party up in the rafter,
With giggles and laughter.
The cats watch in vain,
While birds take the lane.

They dance on the edge,
No fear of the ledge.
With a wink and a grin,
Let the chaos begin!

Nature's Palette on High

Colors splatter and play,
As the skies turn to clay.
Splashed with hues so bright,
It's a comical sight.

Balloons float on the breeze,
While candy grows on trees.
Lemons wink in the sun,
Nature's party is fun.

Blues giggle from the brook,
While the moles read a book.
Butterflies swirl around,
In a colorful sound.

Whimsical critters cheer,
As friends gather near.
With splashes and spins,
The palette begins!

Climbing Toward the Green Abyss

Up we go, grab a vine,
Swinging high, feeling fine.
The trees talk in whispers,
As we play with the sisters.

Kangaroos join the line,
Sipping juice from a pine.
With a hop and a skip,
We're all on this trip.

In the maze of the leaves,
We sneak past the thieves.
They're robbing the nests,
In their silly little vests.

A leap and a shout,
Avoiding the clout.
Down we tumble, round and round,
In laughter, we're bound!

A Symphony from Above

Up in the rafters, a band,
With a drummer and a grand.
Each note sends us spinning,
In wild ways, grinning.

The cat tries to join in,
With a thump and a spin.
But the birds take the stage,
In a feathery rage.

A trumpet blast of cheer,
As the anthem draws near.
The notes fly on high,
Underneath a blue sky.

The concert's a blast,
With the moments that last.
In the chaos of song,
Where all of us belong!

Shadows of the Overhead Forest

In the attic, squirrels prance,
On a shelf, they take a chance.
They tiptoe past the dusty shoes,
In a world of giggles and silly hues.

A raccoon wearing a colorful hat,
Debates with a mouse about kite and cat.
The ceiling fans swing like leafy trees,
While a lost potato sings with ease.

The Lofty Wilderness

Above the stairs, a party brews,
With parrots chirping and joyful views.
A lion roars, but it's just a toy,
While kids create a ruckus of joy.

The attic's filled with laughter and crumbs,
As creatures march with silly drums.
A bear in pajamas plays on a slide,
In this whimsy, no one can hide.

Tales from the Hidden Heights

In the shadows, a monkey swings,
While a rabbit tells of fanciful things.
They plot and scheme with every whim,
Under the light, they dance and swim.

A hedgehog dreams of a grand parade,
Gathering friends in the brightness that fades.
With confetti made from old paper cups,
They laugh until their giggles erupt.

Birds in the Forgotten Nook

Tucked away, where dust bunnies dwell,
Birds tell tales of a mystical spell.
They flap their wings and wiggle their tails,
As laughter dances like silly scales.

A parrot squawks in a comical tone,
While mice serve cheese on a tiny throne.
The forgotten nook is a vibrant scene,
Where nonsense reigns and joy's evergreen.

Ferns and Fantasies

In the lush of green, they prance and play,
Frogs in tuxedos, hippos on a sleigh.
Sloths with sunglasses lounge in delight,
While squirrel chefs serve acorns each night.

Parrots gossip in a stylish flair,
But watch out, there's a monkey with your hair!
Vines twist like dancers, they're putting on shows,
As the breeze brings secrets that nobody knows.

The View from Above

Perched on a branch, oh what a sight,
Birds in bow ties have a karaoke night.
Squirrels debating who steals the most snacks,
While raccoons build towers with leftover packs.

An owl with glasses reads the latest news,
A challenge to the crows for the best of their blues.
Nature's own circus, they all take their turns,
Each twist and each laugh is what friendship earns.

Urban Serengeti

Lions in traffic, quite out of their zone,
Meerkats juggling their phones on their own.
Pigeons holding court, feathers all in a flurry,
As the city buzzes, none seem in a hurry.

Giraffes peek over buildings so tall,
While zebra baristas serve coffee to all.
At lunchtime, a picnic of crumbs and sweet jams,
With laughter and chaos, the city's true charms.

A Canvas of Canopies

Brushstrokes of green paint the sky so bright,
Critters compose a symphony of delight.
Chameleons play dress-up, such great taste,
While bears with paintbrushes create in haste.

Treetops are canvases, bursting with glee,
As butterflies flutter, a dance to see.
In this vibrant world, where laughter ignites,
The art of the wild brings all sorts of sights.

Swaying in the Upper Chambers

In a room where vines take flight,
Chairs are swaying, oh what a sight!
A monkey steals my snack with glee,
He dances on the TV, whee!

My plants are chatting, loud and clear,
They're gossiping, hold your ear!
The ceiling fan, a rotor queen,
Twirls with grace, a true machine!

Nature's Serenade Above

Can you hear the playful tune?
A frog is croaking like a loon!
A parrot rehearses jokes to share,
In the living room, beyond compare!

The windows snagged with leafy greens,
Reflect a world of silly scenes.
The curtain sways, a dancer bold,
With stories of mischief, yet untold.

The Brush of Wings in the Air

A butterfly flaps with flair,
Drawing giggles from the air.
It lands atop the lamp to rest,
A tiny king in feathered vest!

The neighbors hear a happy song,
As critters gather, big and strong.
Each critter wears a funny hat,
And listen to the wise old cat.

Enchanted Heights

In a nook where laughter soars,
The ceiling's painted with funny roars.
A snail claims it as his own,
Taking hours to make it known!

The clock strikes noon with a silly chime,
The sun winks down, it's party time!
Up here, in this whimsical place,
Life's a game, full of grace!

When Walls Become Wilderness

In a room where plants have grown,
The cat thinks he owns this throne.
Vines twist and climb, oh what a sight,
While I search for my shoe, lost in the night.

The fridge, a cave where snacks reside,
I tiptoe past, can't let them hide.
There's a parrot that squawks with glee,
Could he be planning a rescue for me?

A ladder leads up to the ceiling high,
I swear the curtains could almost fly.
Fairies might dance where the dust bunnies dwell,
Or is that just my imagination's spell?

With every creak, the house might laugh,
Maybe it plays at a jungle giraffe.
And if a lion should roar from the hall,
I'll just offer him chips and hope for a brawl.

Lush Dreams Unfurled

My bed transformed to a leafy glen,
Where pillows sprout flowers, and dreams begin.
With bright colors swirling, a circus unfolds,
In this vibrant night, no tales are too bold.

A rabbit in sneakers hops near my toes,
Wearing a hat made from garden hose.
Laughter erupts when he trips on a bloom,
Creating a ruckus that fills up the room.

A swing made of vines hangs from my wall,
I soar over landscapes, so vivid and tall.
With a buddy named Toad who wears little shoes,
We bounce through the forests, singing the blues.

One whisper of breezes, and I feel alive,
In this playful realm where giggles thrive.
If I swing hard enough, hey, maybe I'll fly,
To visit a kingdom beyond the blue sky.

Chasing the Sunbeams

Sunlight spills in like syrupy gold,
I leap for the rays, feeling quite bold.
Dancing around in my socks with flair,
Pretending the floor is a tropical lair.

The sofa's a ship, setting sail on high,
Captured by clouds, we drift through the sky.
With my crew of stuffed bears, we conquer the sea,
Rescuing turtles from peril and glee.

Through windows I'll chase every glimmering light,
A race with the shadows that lurk out of sight.
But my little dog snoozes and dreams on the floor,
While I make my rounds, seeking more and more.

Adventures abound when you're ready to play,
Where sunbeams and laughter can brighten your day.
I'll twirl and I'll spin 'neath the playful sun,
In this silly dance, where all hearts run.

Habitats of the Soul

Where socks are creatures, wild and untamed,
They travel the edges where kindness is claimed.
An old teddy bear holds wisdom profound,
With stories of laughter and joy all around.

In the corner, a dust bunny grins wide,
Knowing secrets and mischief, it cannot hide.
I join in its antics, a whimsical spree,
As we plot tiny schemes, just the dust and me.

Each shelf's a mountain, each drawer a cave,
Full of treasures, like memories to save.
Knickknacks and trinkets hold stories of yore,
Breathing life into dreams we simply adore.

Wall paint can whisper, in colors so bright,
Of galaxies swirling in the hush of the night.
In this haven of laughter, where day meets the soul,
We celebrate whimsies that make us feel whole.

Magpie's Hideaway in the Heights

In the rafters birds conspire,
Chirping secrets, never tire.
A magpie's nest of shiny trinkets,
Amongst the dust, it's quite the linkets.

Feathers tangled with old string,
Squeaks of laughter, chaos they bring.
They argue over who gets the boot,
While trying to fit in a colorful suit.

A dance of shadows, flaps, and flings,
Their beaks a-band for nonsense sings.
The ceiling beams creak with delight,
As mischief brews in the waning light.

When the sun sets, and echoes play,
The chatter hinders the end of the day.
With a wink and a hop, they fly anew,
In this hideaway where fun ensues.

Hushed Murmurs in the Loft

In the corners, whispers float,
Mice get together, planning a boat.
Nibbling crumbs and sharing tales,
While the cat snoozes, with dreamy gales.

A dusty box offers a bed,
From which a wild imagination is fed.
The quiet squeaks turn to laughter's cheer,
As they plot an adventure without any fear.

Old magazines serve as the map,
To navigate without any mishap.
Here we sail on paper seas,
While the neighbor's dog barks, "Oh please!"

Cheese cubes and thimbles, a daring feast,\nThey toast to their fun, and it never ceased.
A gentle night brings dreams to write,
Of tiny escapades that fill up the night.

Canopy of Forgotten Dreams

Underneath a blanket blue,
Wild thoughts sprout from a hidden view.
Laughter dances on gentle streams,
As silly critters chase their dreams.

Crickets play a symphony sweet,
While frogs croak along with their feet.
An old shoe serves as a quirky throne,
For the queen of the loft, who prances alone.

Acorns roll and giggles erupt,
As jays and squirrels crash the cup.
They toast with dew drops, making a cheer,
For another mad adventure that's drawing near.

A wild script on the attic wall,
Tales forgotten and proud, it stands tall.
In the canopy above, where dreams convene,
A world of nonsense, forever unseen.

The Veiled Wilderness Above

In the shadows, night creatures play,
With glowing eyes that seize the day.
A tap on the surface, a rustle, a chirp,
   As the wild parties hide and lurk.

A tangle of vines, a soft bed made,
In plush corners, no fear of shade.
With acrobats swinging from beams of light,
   Their antics are silly, a curious sight.

Pillow fights turn to grand displays,
Down feathers fly in the raucous frays.
Giggling echoes in the muffled gloom,
   Jokes and jests in this cozy room.

As dawn creeps in, the laughter remains,
Of misadventures in whimsical chains.
A wilderness up high, where the fun won't cease,
In a world of nonsense, they find their peace.

Canopy Games in the Upper Spaces

In the loft where squirrels play,
Bouncing high on beams of hay.
Laughter echoes, a wild cheer,
As mischief dances, drawing near.

A parrot mimics all we say,
Juggling nuts in a comical way.
Monkeys swing from rafter to rafter,
Turning idle moments into laughter.

Forgotten toys, a treasure trove,
Finding magic in the grove.
Tangles of string, a cat's delight,
Creating chaos, what a sight!

Beneath the dust, bold secrets thrive,
Bringing the attic, bliss alive.
Each corner holds a silly tale,
Where fun and frolic never pale.

Breaths of the Untamed Above

Breezes brush through hidden spots,
Tickling noses, giving thoughts.
An owl hoots with a wink so sly,
While sleepy bats begin to fly.

Shadows jiggle, shadows jive,
In the attic's heart, we come alive.
Grasshoppers leap from pizza boxes,
Uninvited guests, those little foxes.

Old shoes become puppet shows,
Imagination, where laughter flows.
A dusty globe spins with glee,
As we sail on dreams, wild and free.

Here, in the wilds above our heads,
Wacky antics spread like threads.
Where ordinary is turned about,
With giggles, wiggles, and playful shouts.

The Hidden Bloom of Attic Air

A flower sleeps in an old can,
Dreaming of sunshine, just like a fan.
The attic's warmth, a gentle tease,
As the rogue breeze sways branches and leaves.

Under old books, a critter's den,
Where mischief brews with a wink and grin.
Crickets chirp a concert grand,
Hosting a party, unplanned and unplanned.

A raccoon sneaks for a midnight snack,
Pinching crumbs from a forgotten stack.
A shoelace tied in a funny bow,
Spinning tales that only we know.

So up we go, to play and roam,
In our sanctuary, we find a home.
With every breath, there's joy to share,
In the vibrant dance of attic air.

Sun-Kisses of the High Realm

Golden rays drip like honey sweet,
Shining down where creatures meet.
A raccoon strums on a ukulele,
While shadows chuckle, oh so gaily.

A sunbeam's spotlight on a silly hare,
Dancing wildly without a care.
Socks become capes for brave explorer mice,
Conquering realms of dust, oh so nice!

Giggles echo from a wooden chest,
As toys unite for a fun-filled quest.
Each little nook, a hide-and-seek,
Where laughter reigns, playful and cheek.

Bouncing hearts in the upper glow,
With each moment, adventure does flow.
As sun-kisses paint the world bright,
Every second ignites pure delight.

Ferns and Fables Above

In the corner, ferns take dance,
Whispering secrets with a glance.
A spider spins its silken thread,
While laughing toads play hop instead.

A lizard flaunts its bright green hue,
Thinking it's a parrot too.
With every leap, a tale is spun,
In this realm of mischief and fun.

Beneath the shelf, a cricket jokes,
As sleepy mice recount their hoax.
Each shadow hides a silly plot,
Adding giggles to the lot.

So join this merry crew and see,
The flights of fancy wild and free.
Where fables twist in leafy shade,
And nothing here is ever stayed.

Creatures of the Upper Realm

A squirrel swings from beam to beam,
Chasing shadows in a dream.
With acorns flying, what a sight,
As antics spark from morn till night.

An owl, wise in the daylight gloom,
Winks at mice in living room.
Raccoons wear masks of pure delight,
Planning mischief well past night.

In nooks and crannies, giggles hide,
As beetles scramble, quick to bide.
Each creak and crack brings laughter near,
While critters dance in good cheer.

So peek above and share the peace,
Where every creature's joys increase.
For in this realm of furry charms,
You'll find the joy that always warms.

Wild Wonders Beneath the Eaves

A curly-tailed mouse, oh what a tease,
Pops his head out with such ease.
He's got a plan, a wild scheme,
To steal the cat's delightful cream!

Beneath the eaves, a party brews,
Laughter spills like morning dews.
The ants parade in splendid lines,
And gossip spreads through wooden pines.

A beetle's band kicks off the fun,
With tiny drums, they beat as one.
In every crevice, tales unfold,
With giggles wrapped in joy untold.

So linger low and peek around,
In this delightful, grassy ground.
Where whispers float on breezy trails,
And friendship blooms in tiny tales.

Dreams Amidst the Rafter Leaves

Amongst the rafters, dreams collide,
With silly voices, they confide.
A chorus of giggles fills the air,
While butterflies flit without a care.

An echo of frogs croaks a tune,
Competitions spring up 'neath the moon.
As owls hoot with comical flair,
Strutting proudly without a care.

In this whimsical, leafy place,
The creatures compete in a funny race.
With giggles echoing in joy,
Every creature, a gleeful toy.

So nestle close and take a peek,
At dreams that hide and hardly speak.
For in this world of laughter bright,
Life's little wonders take flight.

Secrets Drenched in Sunlight

In corners where dust bunnies play,
The sun sneaks in to join the fray.
With spaghetti vines making a scene,
I swear they giggle, oh so mean!

Old shoes dance on ceiling beams,
Telling tales of forgotten dreams.
The cat on a perch, looking so grand,
Plotting mischief, oh isn't that bland?

Tales Woven Through the Beams

The rafters squeak with laughter bright,
As mice tell stories all through the night.
With crumbs and crumbs from ages past,
   They feast on legends that never last.

A squirrel swings in a tattered scarf,
   Crafting jokes with a joyous laugh.
Though he's liked by all in those nooks,
He's still just a thief with an eye for books!

The Loft's Leafy Embrace

A pothos plant in a sunbeam's grace,
Chasing shadows, it finds its place.
With laughter from leaves on the wall,
It's the funniest show after all!

With pillows piled like mountains high,
And blankets that flutter, oh my, oh my!
The attic parties never stop,
Where stuffed animals let humor drop.

Forest Echoes in the Attic

Down by the old trunk with tales to tell,
A pillow fort stands like a castle's shell.
Octopus socks, parade at dawn,
Waving their tentacles, what a con!

Creaky hinges sing in delight,
As crumpled maps take adventurous flight.
With whispers of laughter, echoing clear,
A treasure trove of giggles is here!

The Lost Path Above

Up above in the tangled green,
The squirrels play hide and seek,
With branches they joyfully preen,
While birds squawk tales so unique.

A raccoon dons a hat quite dandy,
Prancing around with a little strut,
He claims his throne, all quite randy,
Makes the wise owl say, "What's up?"

Laughter echoes from vines that sway,
As acorns tumble in a rolly fashion,
Chasing away the blues of the day,
With each little gust in a wild passion.

A secret path, oh so absurd,
Where the harmless slip and slide,
All giggles evolve into a bird,
As nature's charm takes us for a ride.

Murmurs from the Silent Grove

In the grove where the shadows dance,
Whispers float on the breeze so light,
Every leaf twirls in a funny trance,
While bugs hold a symposium at night.

A frog croaks jokes with a great big grin,
Next to him, a lizard rolls his eyes,
They giggle at tales of where they've been,
While fireflies twinkle under the skies.

The trees hold secrets, chortles concealed,
As branches shake with raucous delight,
It's a stage where nature is revealed,
And all of the critters ignite the night.

Under the moon, their antics thrive,
From the quietest brush to the loudest roar,
In whispers and chuckles, they come alive,
In a corner of green, behind nature's door.

Spirited Flora Overhead

Up in the canopy, colors explode,
Where flowers gossip, tossing heads high,
Petals flutter in a chaotic mode,
As butterflies laugh and whirl in the sky.

A daisy whispers a pun to a rose,
"Why don't we toss a garden party?"
The tulips chuckle, strike a pose,
Creating their own brand of confetti.

Moss has a dance-off with the ferns,
As vines snicker at the game they play,
A riot of laughter when sapling churns,
They twist and whirl in a bloom ballet.

Their colors collide like a painter's spree,
In this laughter-filled, lively domain,
Each flower knows their roles with glee,
In nature's canvas, no room for mundane.

The Nest of Forgotten Legends

High in the branches, where stories sleep,
Legends weave through the tangled air,
With each twist, a secret to keep,
As critters pause, with a curious stare.

A parrot recycles a tale so old,
While the wise owl hoots in delight,
"Tell me again, what's it like being bold?"
As they all gather 'round for the night.

Echoes of laughter from stories once told,
Ancient myths wrapped in a leafy embrace,
These friendships cherished, never grow cold,
In a cozy nest of giggles and grace.

As tales take flight on the breeze up high,
The past dances into the present's tune,
With each silly story, they all sigh,
In a realm of whimsy beneath the moon.

Flora of the Forgotten Corners

In shadows creep the ferns so sly,
A cactus giggles, oh my, oh my!
Petals do pirouettes, oh what a sight,
Blossoms have parties, every night!

Behind old pots, they hold a ball,
With dandelions and weeds, they call,
A tap dance of vines, how they delight,
In corners forgotten, shining bright!

Mossy hats on rocks, so chic,
The pansies whisper, 'Come join, be unique!'
A daisy wears shades, cool as can be,
In gardens where laughter runs free!

So if you peek in those secret spaces,
You might find a crew with funny faces,
Where nature's own jesters play all day,
In flora's fun realm, come out and stay!

Sunlight in the Hidden Grove

In beams that dance, the shadows play,
Little creatures scamper, hip-hip-hooray!
Sunlight tickles, a cheeky tease,
While squirrels plan tricks with perfect ease.

Caterpillars strut, they think they're cool,
Swinging on branches, breaking the rule,
The shadows laugh, they can't keep still,
In this grove of sunshine, there's always a thrill!

A chirp here, a buzz there, what's that sound?
The mix of laughter, echoing around,
As butterflies giggle, they flit and swirl,
Under this canopy, oh what a whirl!

When daylight dims, the shadows wink,
And in the grove, they chat and think,
With every beam, a tale unfolds,
In sunlight's laughter, life never folds!

Whispers of the Upper Boughs

Above the ground, the whispers soar,
Boughs gossip loudly, who could ask for more?
A parrot's joke, a toucan's grin,
In the branches, fun is always in!

Swaying leaves hold secret schemes,
As monkeys swing through leafy dreams,
With every leap, stories untold,
In the canopy's arms, the laughter unfolds!

"The fruit's too ripe!" a critter shouts,
As friends burst forth with joyful clouts,
In this garden where glee is flair,
Whispers echo with utmost care!

Each rustle and giggle fills the air,
A dance of delight, like a fairground fair,
Take a peek up high, join the fun,
In the upper boughs, adventures run!

The Loft Lush with Life

In a loft that's stuffed with ferns galore,
Lively critters play; what's in store?
With every leaf, a giggle or two,
Life's a party, all green and new!

A spider weaves jokes with silky threads,
While mischievous mice steal crumbs from beds,
Each bubble of laughter rings bright and clear,
In this lively loft, there's nothing to fear!

Oh, come take a stroll through the plush maze,
Where vines twist tales in the sun's warm rays,
The humor blooms in petals wide,
In this lively loft, we're filled with pride!

So pop your head up; don't hesitate,
Join the fun in this lush, lively state,
For in this green haven, every leaf thrives,
And laughter encircles the way that life drives!

Revelations in the Treetops

Squirrels in suits plot with glee,
A meeting of minds in the canopy.
Chatter and banter, a comedic play,
Acorns for snacks in a nutty buffet.

Parrots recite the latest news,
Filling the air with colorful blues.
One says, 'I can juggle a branch!',
While another just falls with a comical ranch.

The monkeys swing by with a jest,
One wears a hat, thinking he's best.
In the heights, laughter echoes loud,
Nature's comedians, oh so proud.

Everyone's laughing, not a care in sight,
As a frog joins in with a leap for delight.
In the treetops, a party unfolds,
With the quirkiest tales nature holds.

Where Nature Meets Barriers

A fence stands tall, what a silly feat,
The birds shake wings and refuse to retreat.
They chirp, 'What's a barrier to the winged?'
They dance 'round the post, freely they sing.

An owl on guard, oh so wise,
With a monocle perched on his eyes.
'You can't cage wisdom,' he starts to chant,
As the rabbits all giggle, 'Oh, you can't!'

Butterflies flutter, sneaking through cracks,
Bringing with them mischievous snacks.
They whisper of joy, whisper of fun,
As nature chuckles under the sun.

Even the leaves join in the game,
'Watch us tumble, it's all the same!'
With laughter that breezes under the stars,
Where barriers crumble, and nature's bizarre.

The Ecosystem of Thought

Ideas grow wild like weeds in the sun,
Twisting and turning, oh what a fun run!
A thought blooms here, a notion pops there,
Ideas chatter gleefully, floating in air.

The wisdom of trees, they hum a tune,
While the flower debates, 'Should I wear a hat, too?'
A beetle chimes in, 'Let's dance in the rain!'
As seeds of laughter burst forth from the grain.

Riddles and puns weave through the grass,
An owl observes, laughing at the sass.
'What's a crow without a good joke?'
While a snake coils up, trying to poke!

In this ecosystem, humor reigns clear,
Where thoughts take flight, and all is sincere.
Join the discussion, it's all quite insane,
In the green of the world, we dance without pain.

Underneath the Branches

Underneath canopies, secrets abound,
Whispers of giggles ricochet 'round.
A raccoon in pajamas searching for loot,
Stumbles on berries, then starts to commute.

A bear rolls by, all fluffy and round,
Slips on a banana, falls straight to the ground.
'What's the rush?' he chuckles, brushing off dirt,
As the squirrel simply laughs, 'Oh, you silly great flirt!'

Twirling about are the leaves in a dance,
To a rhythm so silly, they take a chance.
'Join us!' they beckon from their leafy perch,
While bugs hold a disco, a funny little church.

Beneath the branches, the laughter erupts,
With sunshine and giggles, the fun never corrupts.
Nature's a riot, a joyous spree,
Underneath the branches, come laugh with me!

Reflections of an Untamed Heaven

In a world where parrots squawk with zest,
Monkeys wearing hats are dressed to impress.
Lions sip tea with their pinky in the air,
While zebras joke, pretending they don't care.

The trees are tangled, a messy delight,
Squirrels rehearsing their best acrobat flight.
Frogs in tuxedos hop with great flair,
While owls take selfies, showing off their hair.

Each vine a swing, each leaf a new joke,
Even the hedgehogs try stand-up and poke.
Chameleons changing to match the next pun,
In this wild haven, there's laughter for fun.

So roam through this chaos, embrace every cheer,
In this realm of whimsy, there's nothing to fear.
From trees to the sky, let your spirits lend wings,
For joy is the treasure that nature still brings.

Treasures of the Upper Wilderness

Up in the canopy, curious things roam,
Pirates of the forest, they're far from their home.
A raccoon is trading shiny rocks for snacks,
While turtles attempt to take acrobatic hacks.

The vines weave stories of giggles and fun,
As squirrels engage in a nut-rolling run.
Jaguars in berets paint portraits with grace,
While hedgehogs are mimes, pulling off quite the face.

Beneath leafy umbrellas, the laughter breaks loose,
While chattering birds form a funny truce.
But watch for the sloths, they're slow as can be,
Taking their time for a special cup of tea.

So gather your friends and ascend to the trees,
Join in with the wonders the jungle agrees.
With humor and mischief, let spirits ignite,
In this upper wilderness, everything feels right.

Charm of the Sheltered Grove

In a grove so vivid, where laughter is king,
You'll find creatures giggling at the silliest thing.
A beaver with glasses reads novels on a log,
While crickets compose at twilight like a frog.

The faunas are dancing in whatever tune,
While dancing with shadows beneath the big moon.
Buffalos wearing boots are getting their groove,
And owls, such wise folks, remind us to move.

Each branch is a stage for the wildest of plays,
With critters on set for the longest of days.
Fireflies sparkle like stars caught in a race,
While raccoons perform in a comic embrace.

So come, let us frolic, with joy all around,
In this charming enclave where fun can be found.
Embrace the delight of each silly scheme,
For laughter's a treasure, living out the dream.

Nocturnal Whispers

Under the moon, critters prance,
Furry friends in a midnight dance.
Pigeons plotting their secret plots,
While raccoons steal our leftover thoughts.

Loud owls hoot, but who's the wise?
Squirrels gossip, sharing their lies.
Lions lounging in chaises so grand,
Right atop the bustling land.

Cats trade tales of nine lives spent,
While dogs bark loudly, their voices blend.
A twinkling star throws glittering shade,
On this wild parade, unafraid.

So when you roam under city lights,
Listen close for those wild delights.
In rooftop worlds, laughter swells,
Funny whispers of furry spells.

Overhead Skyscapes

Look above, where eagles soar,
Winking at pigeons, not wanting more.
Parrots squawk, wearing shades of green,
While a sneaky raccoon plays the king.

Kites flutter down, chasing the breeze,
Squirrels debate the best up in trees.
Giraffes peek in through the high-rise glass,
Judging our snacks, oh what a class!

The sun smiles down on this odd display,
As squirrels plot their nutty ballet.
Clouds brush by, like fluffy marshmallows,
While down below, the fun always grows.

So raise a glass to the skies above,
Where wildlife talks of mischief and love.
In our funny world, bizarre and loud,
Let's dance with the critters and feel so proud.

The Forgotten Wild

In alleys dark where shadows creep,
A hedgehog snores, lost in deep sleep.
Lions roam, pretending they're tame,
While cats plot their next greatest game.

Backyards buzz with funky beats,
As ferrets dance in fuzzy retreats.
Trash bins rattle with laughter and cheer,
As raccoons drum with nibbles near.

Frogs croak jokes in melodic tones,
Life's a party in these urban zones.
Hummingbirds dart, stealing the show,
With wings so fast, they put on a glow.

So while we think it's a city so mild,
Beneath it all lies chaos compiled.
Let's join the fun in this playful watch,
In this wild tale, shirtless and botch!

Urban Jungle Chronicles

In the cityscape, the wild runs free,
With lizards sunbathing so carelessly.
Squirrels jump, plotting their grand heist,
Swiping snacks from those who aren't the nicest.

Nights are bustling with funny old tunes,
As raccoons tap dance beneath the moons.
Bats joke around and flit with flair,
Every corner a giggle, a silly affair.

Turtles meander, real slow like,
While flamingos flaunt in their feathered hike.
Pigeons vote on who's the best flyer,
Laughing at faults, they never tire.

So raise your voice to the scenes so bright,
Where humor reigns, and joy takes flight.
In these chronicles of urban delight,
The wild takes charge each fun-filled night.

Adventures in the Loft

In the attic's wild and daring space,
Dust bunnies frolic, quicken the pace.
A sock puppet lion roars with glee,
While raccoons debate on who gets the tea.

Old boxes stacked as towers so bright,
Each creak of the floorboards, a comical fright.
The ghost of the cat naps, purring aloud,
Draped in a blanket, so cozy and proud.

An owl with glasses reads tales to the mice,
While tangled-up vines dance, oh so nice.
An opera of laughter, echoing high,
Where all of our dreams take flight in the sky.

With glowing fireflies lighting the way,
A band of lost toys starts a ballet.
So come one, come all, take a leap with a grin,
In this attic of wonders, let the fun begin!

The Untamed Attic

Beneath the beams where the shadows play,
A scruffy old teddy calls for a stay.
Socks on the ceiling seem stuck in a fight,
While baseball cards scatter, a marvelous sight.

Giraffes made of yarn prance with delight,
On a swing made of dust, they take off in flight.
A parrot in plaid gives pointers on style,
As the wall clock giggles with an eccentric smile.

Crumpled up papers spell out a joke,
A sneaky old raccoon in a hat made of smoke.
Bouncing off walls with giggles and cheer,
The attic's alive, with nothing to fear!

So put on your hat, grab your wildest friend,
Together, let's see where the fun will extend.
Among things forgotten, treasures unrevealed,
In the untamed attic, laughter's the shield.

Whispers of the Canopy

Nooks in the attic hide secrets and tales,
Where echoes of laughter dance in the gales.
Wind chimes are whispering jokes from the past,
As squirrels in pajamas munch nuts, oh so fast!

A chandelier of old toys swings from the beams,
Reflecting the stories of wild childhood dreams.
Teddy bears gossip, knitting up schemes,
Creating hilarity from fantasy themes.

Bouncing on furniture, they leap and they fly,
From corner to corner, oh my, oh my!
Cats in the rafters, with shenanigans rife,
Holding a meeting to discuss their sweet life.

With dancing curtains, and giggles that spread,
It's a carnival of mischief where fun is widespread.
A tapestry woven with laughter and cheer,
In the whispers of wonder, dreams wander near.

Shadows in the Loft

In the shadows where misfits come out to play,
A pirate with flashlights leads the way.
Monkeys in costumes climb up with flair,
Swinging and swirling, without a care!

Old dolls hold court in a mysterious light,
Debating the best snacks for a magical night.
While a tuna can tiptoes, making its plot,
To steal all the snacks that were neatly forgot!

Crisp autumn leaves rustle, make silly sounds,
As ghosts in pajamas tiptoe around.
But no need to worry, for it's all in good fun,
Laughter and joy under the imaginary sun.

To play in the shadows, with whimsy in mind,
No telling the wonders that we'll surely find.
So join in the fun, let your spirit take flight,
In the loft's silly kingdom, it's pure delight!

A Garden Among the Shadows

In a patch of sun, the cat naps low,
A squirrel debates, should he stay or go?
The plants gossip, their secrets abound,
While shadows dance lightly on the ground.

A tomato grumbles, too plump for its skin,
While cucumbers twist in a comical spin.
Beneath the broad leaves, a turtle is seen,
Critiquing the roses for being too green.

A garden party with worms long and slim,
They're jigging and jiving, it's all quite a whim.
The daisies are laughing, they can barely stand,
At the sight of a beetroot wearing a band.

So come take a peek at this festival bright,
Where every odd plant brings a giggle or fright.
In a garden that's tangled and full of delight,
Big laughs grow alongside with each passing night.

Above the Mundane World

Up in the air, the pigeons conspire,
Wings flapping wildly, they dance on a wire.
A parrot is making a speech that's absurd,
While a seagull's busy collecting his birds.

The rooftops are lively, with hats all askew,
Chimney pots grinning, enjoying the view.
A raccoon in shades rides a bike made of cheese,
The alley cats giggle at such oddities.

Each window a world, so silly, so bright,
Curtains are twitching, what a curious sight!
A mop on a mission waltzes by chance,
In the rhythm of life, as the rooftops all dance.

So leap and rejoice in this crazy parade,
Above the dull ground, where wonders are made.
With laughter echoing from each lofty place,
Join the madcap chorus in this silly race!

Flights of the Hidden Spirits

In twilight's embrace, the shadows all twirl,
Whispers of fun start to take on a swirl.
Sprites on their scooters, zooming around,
With giggles that bounce o'er the moonlit ground.

A gnome wearing sneakers trips over a root,
While fairies are crafting sweet melodies—cut!
They float like confetti, all pink and all blue,
Trying to pin down the sounds, but who knew?

The owls in the trees hoot with delight,
Telling tall tales that stretch through the night.
While squirrels on rollerblades spin with such flair,
As laughter erupts from the shimmering air.

So let your heart wander where magic is found,
With spirits that frolic and joy all around.
In the hidden flights where the laughter grows wide,
Unlock the enchantment, let humor be your guide!

Laughter Among the Leaves

A leaf fell down, with a chuckle so loud,
Declaring itself the queen of this crowd.
The branches all leaned in to hear the tale,
As the breeze brought whispers of a cheeky gale.

A raccoon in a vest, tipsy from fruit,
Struts through the thicket, all swanky and cute.
Trees swing their branches, applauding the scene,
While bushes are roaring, what a raucous machine!

Mice play the drums on a hollowed old log,
Setting the rhythm, a swing for the fog.
And crickets join in with their chirps of delight,
Creating a symphony that brightens the night.

So let's dance with abandon, chortling away,
In this wild tapestry where critters at play.
Where laughter and leaves fuse in joyous spree,
In the heart of the forest, let's all just be free!

Flight of the Feathered Mind

In the attic there's a crow,
Telling tales of high and low.
His beak's a quiver, full of glee,
What nonsense flies from him, you see!

Socks and shoes all out of place,
He insists they have a race.
Pigeons cheer as he takes flight,
What a sight, oh what a sight!

Lampshades dance, the dust will twirl,
As crumbs of laughter make a swirl.
With every flap, he tells a joke,
And still, he thinks he's quite the bloke!

So if you hear a little squawk,
Join in the fun, have a little talk.
For upstairs there's a party wild,
With a crow who's a foolish child!

Hidden Dwellers Within

Beneath the floorboards, something stirs,
A family of mice with fuzzy furs.
They hold a feast on crumbs galore,
And do a dance, then ask for more!

One wears a hat, another a tie,
They tip their hats as you pass by.
With silly pranks and merry laughs,
They keep their secrets in the drafts.

A game of hide and squeak ensues,
With every chase, they're all confused.
Nibbles of cheese and bits of bread,
Who could have dreamt this could be said!

So if you hear a tiny squeak,
Just know it's fun, not scary freak.
For in our homes, the little crew,
Turns daily life into a zoo!

Roots of Contemplation

In pots and drums, the plants convene,
A funky garden, quite the scene.
With roots that wiggle, leaves that sway,
They ponder life in their own way.

The cacti joke about their prick,
While ferns tell tales that need a flick.
They sip on sunlight, breathe in air,
And gossip softly, unaware.

With every growth, a thought expands,
As daisies debate with waving hands.
What is the purpose? What's the plan?
In the land of pots, the fun began.

So if you see them dancing bright,
Just know they ponder day and night.
For roots and stems, in silly talk,
Create a world that makes us balk!

The Serpent's Path

A wiggly snake up on the stair,
Slithers 'round without a care.
He wears a hat that's way too big,
And thinks he's cool as he does a jig.

He curls around the banister tight,
Sings songs that give his pals a fright.
With every twist, a joke appears,
The other critters giggle near.

"Life's a path that bends and sways,
Like my body through the rays!"
He winks and wiggles, full of cheer,
Bringing smiles, and never fear!

So if you find him on your way,
Join the fun, don't shy away.
For laughter coils like he does too,
In his merry world, just for you!

The Loft of Forgotten Flora

In the attic where curious vines grow,
Potted plants giggle, they put on a show.
A cactus wearing glasses, oh what a sight,
Chortles with daisies, they dance through the night.

A yucca and fern in a awkward debate,
Argue who's greener, now isn't that great?
Spider plants giggling, they love a good jest,
While rubber trees chuckle, they think they're the best.

Cracks in the ceiling, like laughter, they spread,
Wandering critters, they dive into bed.
A raccoon with a top hat, sipping on tea,
Claims it's a party, come join! Don't be free!

In this wild little corner, chaos reigns true,
With puns and old potted plants waiting for you.
We're lost in this attic, where fun never ends,
Just watch for the roots—they're sneaky, my friends!

Serpentine Shadows in the Loft

In the corner, a snake with a taste for toast,
Claims it's a chef, proud of his boast.
The shadows are wriggling, a comical dance,
While the old dusty boxes just seem to prance.

A lizard in heels struts across the floor,
Says, 'Fashion is key in the loft's grand galore!'
With a wink from the cork, they sip on spilled rum,
Laughing at echoes, they vibrate and hum.

The shadows emerge, and they whisper a plot,
To spin the old tales that they've long forgot.
They giggle and writhe, while munching on cheese,
What a riot it is to just hang in the breeze!

In this serpentine play where the oddity gleams,
Time wanders slowly, dancing with dreams.
Each shadow a character, a riotous spree,
Come join this adventure, oh won't you agree?

The Wilds of Higher Ground

Up in the rafters, where the wild things play,
There's an owl who can rap and a parrot ballet.
Funky old moths busting out their best moves,
Spreading cheer in the chaos, it's what they approve.

A squirrel in pajamas makes a fan club tonight,
While a hedgehog named Steve is ready to write.
With acorns for pens, they scribble and jest,
As the attic's a stage for the party, no rest!

Vines swing like dancers, rocks wear a grin,
The wilds of the loft draw everyone in.
Each nook and each cranny tells tales on the wall,
Of mischief and laughter, they beckon us all.

So come raise a glass to this rambunctious crew,
To the wonders and witticisms waiting for you.
In the wilds of heights where the odd never sleeps,
The hilarity echoes, and the joy never weeps!

Flights of Fancy Above

Above the noise, there's a flurry of wings,
A falcon in spectacles, he croons and he sings.
With chatter of sparrows, they cackle and jest,
Laughing at life as if it's a fest.

They swoop and they dive, a comical scene,
Where owls tell tall tales caught in a screen.
With feathers and giggles, the air full of cheer,
It's a raucous assembly, oh, how they revere!

The light streaming down paints their antics in gold,
As they flap around stories all waiting to be told.
Each creature a character, in orbit they swirl,
As the attic's their stage, let the fun unfurl!

So join in the flights of fancy and jest,
For the wild in the rafters is simply the best.
A highflying circus with whimsy in tow,
Let's giggle and soar, let our laughter just flow!

The Ceiling of Greenery

In a room where ferns sway,
The ivy thinks it's on display.
A little bird tweets from above,
Sipping tea, dreaming of love.

The chandelier's a sticker plant,
With branches so bold, they dare to chant.
Lampshades ripe with vines and blooms,
Make the living room feel like tombs.

Cushions hide the playful frogs,
Leaping wild through loose sorted logs.
A polka-dot snail slides on by,
Wearing a hat, oh my, oh my!

Laughter mixes with the leaf,
As plants gossip beyond belief.
In this nook, all's a bit absurd,
A leafy crowd without a word.

Roar Beneath the Floor

Do you hear that clumsy thud?
Or is it just a playful bud?
A tiger's spot beneath the chair,
You'd think it's got a reason to care!

The carpet shudders, all are meek,
Beneath our feet, a lion's squeak.
Oh dear, what happens when you tread?
A pirate's ship beneath your bed?

With every creak, a giggle sounds,
Imaginary creatures abound.
They play tag with the dust bunnies,
While I just trip o'er their funnies.

So let your toes just dance and prance,
While hidden beasts enjoy the chance.
Their roars inspire an avant-garde,
Noisy parties in the backyard!

A Symphony of Leaves

Listen close, what do you hear?
A concert held right in the sphere.
The leaves whistle tunes on the breeze,
Playing songs beneath the trees.

Moss is the drummer, so robust,
Beating out a rhythm, oh what a must!
Crickets chirp, a wild affair,
Join the encore, if you dare!

Sap is dripping, a sweet encore,
Fill the air with sticky galore.
A parrot sings a silly rhyme,
While we sway, without a dime.

Nature's band, both loud and proud,
Singing songs that entertain the crowd.
In this green hall, let laughter soar,
With every note, we laugh some more!

Creatures of the Mind

Close your eyes, what do you see?
Silly beasts from history.
A dancing bear in a top hat,
Just lost his beat, how 'bout that?

Giraffes knitting with their necks,
While hippos play on jungle decks.
Each thought's a creature of its own,
With floppy ears and silly tone.

Tigers roller-skate in a spin,
While monkeys sneak snacks from within.
An elephant paints a colorful scene,
With colors bright and quite obscene.

In this realm that's oh so grand,
Imaginary friends take a stand.
Where everything's funny, light, and free,
Creatures of the mind, just don't flee!

Echos of the Verdant Veil

In a room where plants can play,
Vines twist and twirl in a sunny ballet.
A parrot trying out for a stand-up show,
Cracks jokes about the housecat below.

Laughter bounces off the leafy green,
Where a squirrel's been sighted, oh so keen!
He hoards old socks like they're treasure,
In this green kingdom, fun is the measure.

There's a fern that grooves to a funky beat,
While the spiders are busting out moves on repeat.
A lizard named Larry tells tales of zest,
In this jungle of joy, life's simply the best!

When shadows dance as the day starts to wane,
The laughter lingers, a sweet refrain.
Amidst the chaos, a harmony flows,
In the verdant veil where hilarity grows.

Stories Wrapped in Ivy

Ivy creeps up, a storyteller bold,
Whispering secrets that never get old.
A frog claims his throne on a pile of old shoes,
And croaks out the news like he's on the six o'clock views.

Caterpillars gossip, rolling in glee,
While a raccoon finds his great legacy.
He trades shiny wrappers for tales of surprise,
In a world where laughter is the ultimate prize.

The ceiling fan spins, a wind of delight,
Stirring up giggles that soar in flight.
As chattering birds join in the fun,
Life's rich tapestry, oh what a run!

Each nook and cranny tells tales galore,
Of mischief and mayhem, laughter at the core.
In this ivy jungle, stories unfold,
Wrapped in humor, forever retold.

The Attic's Untamed Heart

In the attic above, the wild things roam,
With dust bunnies forming a league of their own.
A raccoon and a fox host a card game there,
While the old trunk hums its sweet, storied air.

Against the walls, cobwebs spin their yarn,
With tales of mischief, crafted with charm.
The owls give out wisdom, wrapped up in night,
While all the old toys begin to delight.

Squeaky mice mingle with vintage decor,
Chasing each other while the attic roars.
A jack-in-the-box bursts, oh, what a thrill,
As laughter erupts and echoes the chill.

This untamed heart, so lively and spry,
Under the eaves, where imagination can fly.
In every corner, a sparkle, a quip,
In this attic of wonders, let's never skip!

Lush Lore Above the Dust

Above the clutter, where shadows play,
The tales take flight and dance all day.
An old gnome perched on a shelf with a grin,
Tells riddles to whoever pulls the pin.

The cardboard box becomes a beast,
Disguised as a castle for a tea-party feast.
With stuffed animals wriggling in glee,
And cookies that vanish mysteriously.

A dusty old lamp joins the laughter parade,
Swinging its light like it's not afraid.
Sipping on sunshine, hoarding giggles galore,
This lush lore above, who could ask for more?

In the heights where whispers tickle the air,
Every cranny and nook hides a funny affair.
So remember this place, so endless and bright,
Where stories and laughter lift spirits to flight.

www.ingramcontent.com/pod-product-compliance
Lightning Source LLC
Chambersburg PA
CBHW070305120526
44590CB00017B/2564